Seriously Sweet & Savory

Ketogenic-based recipes; hassle free with all the flavor

By

Dawn Martin

Alex Jammali

Seriously Sweet & Savory

Ketogenic-based recipes; hassle free with all the flavor

Dawn Martin

Alex Jammali

Copyright 2017 by Dawn Martin and Alex Jammali

ISBN-13: 978-0-9997733-0-7

Bonduel, WI

Table of Contents:

Introduction...12

Meet the team..14

What do I need?...16

   Equipment That You Will Need..16

Just to Make Things Easier:...17

   Quick and Easy Sweet Potato Puree...17

   Quick and Easy Pear Puree...18

   Quick and Easy Pumpkin Puree..18

   Watch Your Flours..18

Breads...20

   Chocolate Zucchini Bread-Naturally..22

   Cinnamon-Pecan "Rolls"..24

Cakes..26

   Chocolate Cake...28

   Raspberry Drizzle...30

   Orange Drizzle...30

Decadent Chocolate Cake..32

Fruit Sauce...33

German Chocolate Birthday Cake..34

Coconut-Pecan Frosting...35

Pound Cake..36

Strawberry Torte Cake...38

Carrot Cake...40

Cream Cheese Frosting...41

Frosting..42

Chocolate Buttercream Frosting..44

Dairy-Free Chocolate Fudge Frosting...44

Chocolate Butter Frosting...45

Candy..46

Chocolate Cherry Walnut Fudge..48

Honey Peanut Crunchers..50

Dairy-Free Mint Fudge..52

Mocha Truffles...54

Peanut Butter Balls..56

Cookies..........58

- Pecan-Oatmeal Chocolate Chip Cookies..........60
- Pecan-Oat Raw Cookies..........62
- Raspberry Thumbprints..........64
- Chocolate Nibblers..........66
- P.B. & J Cookies..........68
- Almond Cookies (Bird Seed Cookies)..........70
- "Sugar" Cookies..........72
- Fruit Pizza..........74
- Chocolate Chip Cookies..........76
- Gingerbread Cookies..........78

Desserts..........80

- Chocolate Coconut Mousse..........82
- Lemon Lime Curd..........84
- Fudge Brownies..........86
- Fudge Brownie Frosting..........86
- Chocolate Pudding..........88
- Vanilla Pudding..........90

Ice Cream: 92
- Peach Ice Cream............94
- Chocolate Almond Dairy-Free Ice-Cream............96
- Mint-Chocolate Chip Ice Cream............98
- Vanilla Ice Cream............100
- Banana Fudge Swirl............102
- Fudge............102
- Banana Ice-Cream............104
- Strawberry Ice-Cream............104
- Raspberry Ice-Cream............105
- Pineapple-Orange-Mango............106
- Chocolate Cherry Truffle Ice Cream............108
- Hot Fudge Sauce............110
- Chocolate Almond Ice-Cream............112

Muffins and Scones............114
- Apple Walnut Muffins............116
- Pumpkin-Raisin Muffins............118
- Orange-Cranberry Muffins............120

Pecan-Apricot Scones..122

Oatmeal-Raisin Scones..124

Pies...126

Apple Galatte...128

Bing Cherry Pie..130

Chocolate Raspberry Cheesecake Pie...132

Lemon-Lime Pie...134

Peach-Blueberry Crisp with Maple Balsamic..136

Crusts...138

Roll-out Pie Crust..140

Almond Pie Crust..141

Chocolate Pie Crust..142

Meringue Pie Crust...143

Savory..144

Oatmeal-Garlic Cheddar Biscuits..146

Pizza..148

Garlic Parmesan Crackers...150

Pancakes..152

Berry Chutney...152

Snacks:...154

Plain Granola..156

Chocolate Cherry Granola..158

Sweet and Spicy Trail Mix...160

Cranberry Flax Granola Bars...162

Chocolate Cherry Granola Breakfast Bars..164

Jamie's Granola Bar..166

Introduction:

Why should anyone write a cookbook? Hasn't it all been done already? Despite the internet and the shelves of cookbooks already available, I decided to throw my hat into the ring. I have a good friend that kept telling me to write this cookbook. I tried ignoring her but that didn't work. So Vickie M., thanks for the encouragement and belief in me.

Vickie M. might have been the catalyst but my husband is the inspiration behind this book. You see, he has some health problems that weren't cured with medication, and surgery was a poor option. We realized that we still had another option. The food we put into our bodies.... It could help heal us or hurt us.

After much research, we changed our diet to be sugar and mostly grain free. We were hoping to stop and possibly reverse the growth of the tumor in my husband's brain. Although the tumor remains (but isn't growing at this time), we were surprised by the other benefits of changing what we ate. This is what we experienced: weight loss (my husband 50 pounds, myself 25), my husband no longer has sleep apnea, we no longer crave sweets, we don't experience blood sugar spikes and drops, we don't have the afternoon low where you are searching for anything to give you energy (caffeine, sweets), increase in energy, and lastly FOOD TASTES BETTER! Can you imagine a sweet pepper that tastes sweet? I always wondered why they were called sweet peppers; I didn't think they were sweet before.

The recipes that follow are a result of modifying old favorites and creating brand new favorites. Some of the recipes you will enjoy immediately and others will be those that you develop an enjoyment for. It all depends on how much sugar and grain you are still eating. These recipes were developed with the non-sugar, non-grain eater in mind. The recipes are tasty, fortifying, and indulgent. You may find that you only need a small portion because they are so rich and satisfying. Best of all, they are a much healthier choice. These treats are packed full of protein instead of empty calories. You may want to start with the ones that use some honey as they will be closer to what you are used to. As you become accustomed to less sweetness, the other ones will satisfy.

As you start your adventure in changing how you eat, I have a few recommendations that worked for me. Step one: decide you are changing what you eat not "going without". Sounds silly but this can be a big stumbling block. I didn't succeed until I had things I liked to eat... that's how these recipes have helped me. Step two: read labels. Don't eat things with sugar and grain. Not easy but it can be done. Break it down so it isn't so overwhelming. We started with high fructose corn syrup and once we mastered that went on to add the sugar and grain. Some people can go cold turkey. That works too! Be ready for some unpleasant side effects. I forgot to mention that to my friend Kathy...sorry! Headaches are common as are aches, and no motivation. This will pass and you will feel better for it. Keep in mind that I am not a doctor and I am sharing my experience. You should consult your doctor if you have any questions or concerns.

Meet the team:

As with any large project, I did not do this alone. My niece, Alex, has become my partner in this endeavor. She is a gifted photographer and a visual artist. It doesn't hurt that she has loads of food allergies either! Many of the foods that were off limits to her before are available again with these recipes. I create the recipes while she makes them shine.

What would a cookbook be without testers? I have 4 built-in taste testers. My children have suffered through the failures and tasted the "just desserts" of success. You would think that children can't eat like this... they just won't stand for it! Oh, contraire mon frère: they actually like these recipes and prefer them to others. They still eat birthday cake at parties and snacks at the movies, but it is all about how much and how often. I am hoping to spare them the health problems that follow a lifetime of eating poorly. We also have a large extended family and I have been blessed with great friends. All of whom, gave me honest, helpful feedback on the recipes during development. I will quote one of my friends here, "Those cookies on the back of the plate? What were they? They were just awful!" Needless to say, that recipe in its original context is not in the book thanks to her suffering taste buds.

And last but certainly not least, I need to include Abby. My technical editor extraordinaire! Abby worked tirelessly to not only test recipes but to also type, edit, and compile this book. Abby was the new energy that helped us bring the book to completion. I could not have done it without you Abby! In the process of making a cookbook, she learned tons of patience....lost or unsaved files, having an Aunt that works on the wrong file, and a slow, slow, slow, twisted laptop to work with. Well done Rosie!

Please try these recipes. Buying the book is great, but using it is better. Many of the recipes have just a few ingredients and easy directions. I have tried to use a format that works. When I try something new, I like it in simple, easy to use terms. Life is busy and complicated; these recipes are not.

What do I need?

So you have read my fun and informative introduction... if you haven't I promise not to take the book back. You are thinking of tasty, healthy treats and it is time to bake! Only you just discovered that you don't have half of what you need. I am including an equipment list to help you get organized.

Equipment That You Will Need

Mixer (handheld or stand)

Food Processor (if you plan to grind your own nuts, a must; otherwise wish list)

Blender (for many of the recipes you can get away with a blender if you don't have a food processor, but put the food processor on your wish list)

Ice-cream maker (sounds like a huge investment but they aren't expensive. You can get a decent one for $40-$60. I got mine for $5 at a tag sale)

Just to Make Things Easier:

When it comes time to bake, I am ready to bake! I don't want to use that time for prepping. I have a few tips that make baking more fun.

You will find sweet potato puree and pear puree in many of my recipes. I prepare the purees in bulk batches and freeze them in plastic freezer bags. I will put in say ½ cup of sweet potato because that is the measurement I need for many recipes. Pears will normally be a cup for the same reason. I pull the bags out of the freezer and let them thaw while I start the recipe. If you are in a hurry, place them in warm water for a few minutes and that will speed-up the thawing.

Buying in season and freezing a bunch also reduces your cost. The food tastes better too! Of course, you don't have to do it this way. You can make your purees as part of the baking process. That will just add some time to the recipe. Do what works best for you.

Quick and Easy Sweet Potato Puree

Scrub sweet potato. Place on parchment lined baking sheet. Bake at 350° until soft, around 30-60 minutes. Let cool until you can handle them. Peel and put in blender or food processor. Process until smooth. Package in bags and freeze. Don't forget to label them.

> **Tip:** When I batch bake a bunch of sweet potatoes, I plan to have them for supper too. I just bake up a couple extra and I have my side dish ready. I started doing this because the house smelled so good that everyone wanted to eat the potatoes I was baking to puree.

Quick and Easy Pear Puree

Wash and peel pears. Cut into chunks. Place in blender or food processor. Process until smooth. Package and label. Put into freezer.

> **Tip:** I lay the bags flat in the freezer then stand them up later after they are frozen. This makes it faster to thaw them later, and also saves freezer space, and they are easier to stack than big "lumps."

Quick and Easy Pumpkin Puree

Making pumpkin puree is not as hard as it sounds. Actually, it is rather easy. You will need the small pie pumpkins for a tasty puree. Cut the pumpkin in half, scoop out the seeds and scrap the stringy inside out. Place halves on a parchment lined cookie sheet. Fill each half with some water, about ¼ cup. Cover with a piece of parchment paper. You can also just put them cut side down on the parchment. Either way will work. Bake in a 350° oven until the pumpkin is soft and tender. Let cool slightly. Scrape the warm pumpkin out of the rind and into a blender or food processor. Process until smooth. Scoop into freezer bags. I put into 2 cups per bags. Don't forget to label the bags. Lay bags flat in your freezer (a very important step, otherwise you get big, orange lumps!). That folks is all it takes.

Watch Your Flours

When you are making the recipes, watch the flours. There is a difference between almond flour and blanched almond flour. Almond flour will give the recipe a nuttier flavor while blanched almond flour is off-white, smoother almost like flour from grains. The blanched almond flour will give your recipe a closer resemblance to foods made with grain flours.

"Mistakes are the portals of discovery."

-James Joyce

Breads

If you have a garden you understand zucchini recipes. These plants produce like crazy and we need to find a way to use them. Out in the country, we start locking our car and house doors around the middle to end of summer... not for safety though. We are trying to prevent friends and family from dropping off their extra zucchini! But if they manage to drop it off, you can use it to make this tasty, moist bread.

Shopping List:

1. Prunes
2. Zucchini
3. Canola Oil
4. Eggs
5. Sweet Potato Puree
6. Almonds
7. Oatmeal
8. Baking Soda
9. Salt
10. Baking Powder
11. Cocoa Powder
12. Walnuts

Chocolate Zucchini Bread-Naturally

16 prunes
½ cup water

Combine in saucepan. Cook on low for 5 minutes or until prunes soften. Using a cover will speed up the process. Puree in blender or food processor.

1 cup shredded zucchini
¼ cup canola oil
2 eggs
¾ cup sweet potato puree

Add zucchini, oil, eggs, and sweet potatoes to pureed prunes in food processor or place in mixing bowl. Blend until combined.

1 cup almonds, ground
½ cup oatmeal, ground
½ tsp. baking soda
¼ tsp. salt
¼ tsp. baking powder
½ cup cocoa powder
½ cup chopped walnuts

Combine ground almonds, oatmeal, baking soda, salt, baking powder, cocoa powder in a bowl. Add to zucchini mixture. Blend until combined, scraping down bowl. Add walnuts and mix just until combined.

Not every recipe has a story, but this one has a great one: My sister, Chris, was visiting. Although she has many food restrictions in her diet, Chris loves chocolate. As I was planning breakfast, I thought I would make cinnamon rolls for everyone and chocolate brownies for her. We all sat down and ate our eggs and such. Coffee was poured and it was time for the bakery! My family waited in gleeful anticipation (I am kind-of known for the food I make), I unveiled the sticky buns for the majority and the brownies for Chris. Chris says, "Oh, I don't get sticky buns?" I respond, "You love chocolate." She hangs her head slightly, and mumbles, "Yah, I do." By her body language, I can tell she is extremely disappointed... I learned something that day. Chris loves cinnamon rolls more than chocolate on Saturday mornings. I developed this recipe so I never have to see her disappointed face again. This one is for you Chris!

Shopping List:

1. Earth Balance
2. Pecans
3. Honey
4. Cinnamon
5. Blanched Almond Flour
6. Coconut Flour
7. Sea Salt
8. Baking Soda
9. Xanthan Gum
10. Yeast
11. Vanilla
12. Egg

Cinnamon-Pecan "Rolls"

You may substitute regular butter for Earth Balance in this recipe.

Roll topping:
6 tsp. Earth Balance, heaping
⅓ cup pecans, chopped
1 Tbsp. honey
1 tsp. cinnamon

Grease 6 spots in a muffin tin. Add 1 tsp. of Earth Balance, some of the honey, pecans and cinnamon to each spot. Set aside.

Dough:
1 cup blanched almond flour
1 Tbsp. coconut flour
⅛ tsp. sea salt
¼ tsp. baking soda
¼ tsp. xanthan gum

Combine the almond flour, coconut flour, salt, baking soda, xanthan gum in bowl. Set aside.
1 tsp. warm water
⅛ tsp. yeast

In a cup, mix yeast and water. Set aside.

2 Tbsp. honey
1 tsp. vanilla
1 egg
4 Tbsp. Earth Balance
Extra Earth Balance for buttering parchment

In mixing bowl, combine honey, vanilla, egg, Earth Balance. Add yeast mixture. Mix. Add flour mixture. Mix until blended, scraping down the bowl. Using Earth Balance, butter a 9" x 13" or larger piece of parchment paper. Spread dough on buttered parchment into a 7" x 11" rectangle. Using a rubber spatula makes this easier.

Filling inside roll:
1 tsp. cinnamon
1 tsp. Earth Balance; heaping
1 tsp. honey

Keeping away from the edges, sprinkle 7" x 11" rectangle of dough with cinnamon. Drizzle on honey. Dab on Earth Balance. Roll dough into a log. Pickup parchment and use it to "roll" the dough into log. Press long edge gently to seal together. Cut into 6 pieces. Place into prepared muffin tin. Press roll slightly so it fills the tin to the sides. Bake 325° for 8 minutes. Cover with foil then bake at 325° for 7 more minutes. Flip onto a tray. Scrape out toppings onto rolls. Serve warm.

Tip: The recipe can be made ahead and frozen. Just warm slightly in oven. Yummy!

(Pictured at the beginning of this section)

Cakes

Tip: Many of these recipes contain honey. You can increase the amount a little to increase the sweetness if you need to. We try to keep sweeteners like honey, juice, dried fruit and jelly to a very small part of our diet. Remember dessert is still dessert... eat in moderation.

Shopping List:

1. Butter
2. Eggs
3. Honey
4. Milk
5. Blanched Almond Flour
6. Coconut Flour
7. Cocoa Powder
8. Baking Soda
9. Baking Powder
10. Salt
11. Xanthan Gum

If you have a good chocolate cake recipe, it makes you feel like you have it all. This recipe is easy to make and will meet your chocolate craving head-on!

Chocolate Cake

Wet Ingredients:
¾ cup butter
3 eggs
½ cup honey
1 cup milk

In a mixing bowl, beat butter until fluffy. Add honey and mix. Add eggs, 1 at a time. Mix after each egg.

Dry Ingredients:
2 cups blanched almond flour
2 Tbsp. coconut flour
¾ cup cocoa powder
1 tsp. baking soda
¾ tsp. baking powder
¼ tsp. salt
1 tsp. xanthan gum

Mix dry ingredients together in bowl. Add flour mixture alternating with milk to wet ingredients. Beat to combine.

Pour into greased and floured pan or paper-lined muffin tin. Bake at 325° for 10-15 minutes.

(For **mini cupcakes** bake 15 minutes at 325° using silicone pan)

Raspberry Drizzle

1 Tbsp. cream cheese, softened
1 Tbsp. raspberry jelly (100% fruit)
Milk

Either whisk by hand or blend with mixer, cream cheese and jelly. Add just enough milk to make the drizzle slightly runny. Drizzle over cakes or cookies.

Makes enough for 12 mini cupcakes.

Shopping List:

1. Cream Cheese
2. Raspberry Jelly
3. Milk

Orange Drizzle

1 Tbsp. salted butter, melted
1 tsp. orange juice concentrate (frozen oj without adding the water)
Water

Mix orange juice and butter together. Add just enough water to make the drizzle slightly runny. Drizzle over cakes or cookies.

Makes enough for 12 mini cupcakes.

> **Tip:** You can substitute Earth Balance for the butter to make a dairy-free drizzle.

Shopping List:

1. Butter
2. Orange Juice Concentrate

O.K., if I had to pick my very favorite recipe in this book I think it would be this one. It is the very first recipe that I developed using healthier ingredients. It is the one that kicked off the cookbook. Everyone in my family said YUM! It is so good that when I make it there is enough for everyone to have 2 pieces each...we put our names on our second piece in the fridge so nobody else swipes it! This cake is fancy enough for anniversaries and holidays. A small piece goes a long way because it is so rich. Enjoy!

Decadent Chocolate Cake

Special equipment needed: 9" spring form pan. If you do not have one, you can use a 9" cake pan. You just won't be able to display the cake as nicely, because you can't take the whole thing out of the pan at once...think cheesecake for the look of it.

1 pint heavy whipping cream

Beat until peaks form. Set aside in the refrigerator to put on top of finished cake.

18 prunes
½ cup water

Cook prunes and water in a small covered saucepan until soft. Puree while warm. You may need to add just a little warm water to get a smooth, thick puree. Set aside to put on top of finished cake.

Shopping List:

1. Heavy Whipping Cream
2. Prunes
3. 100% Cacao Chocolate Bar
4. Unsalted Butter
5. Instant Coffee
6. Vanilla
7. Almond Flour
8. Sweet Potato Puree
9. Salt
10. Flax
11. Eggs

Shopping List:

1. Unsweetened Blueberries
2. Unsweetened Raspberries
3. Unsweetened Tart (pie) Cherries

Tip: No need to wash the food processor at this point. Just move on to the rest of the recipe...you will use it again. Less cleanup this way.

8 oz. 100 % cacao chocolate (good quality baking chocolate)
¾ cup unsalted butter (1 ¼ sticks)
1 tsp. instant coffee

Place ingredients in pan. Over low heat, melt while stirring constantly. Set aside.

1 tsp. vanilla
1 cup almond flour
1 ½ cups sweet potato puree
¼ tsp. salt
2 Tbsp. flax
4 extra large egg yolks (beat the whites separately until forms peaks)

Combine in food processor. Add melted chocolate mixture. Combine. Fold into beaten egg whites. Pour into greased spring form pan. Bake at 350° for 25 minutes. Remove from pan after cake has cooled some. Spread pureed prunes on cake while it is still warm. After cake is completely cooled, top with whipped cream. Serve on top of a generous helping of fruit sauce. Delicious!

Fruit Sauce

6 cups unsweetened blueberries (frozen is fine)
2 cups unsweetened raspberries
1 ½ cups unsweetened tart (pie) cherries
½ cup water

Place fruit and water in pan. Bring to a boil and reduce heat, stirring often to prevent scorching. Cook until thickened. Cool.

This is Jamie's Birthday Cake but I thought you would like more information in the name. I have been baking German Chocolate Cake for his birthday for ten years or more. We really look forward to his birthday... this cake is fantastic!

German Chocolate Birthday Cake

Wet Ingredients:
4 oz. unsweetened chocolate, premium baking bar
½ cup water
4 eggs, separated
1 cup coconut oil
1 cup coconut milk
1 tsp. vanilla

Dry Ingredients:
2 cups blanched almond flour
½ cup coconut flour
2 tsp. xanthan gum
1 tsp. baking soda
½ tsp. salt

Combine chocolate and water in saucepan. Melt. Cool. Beat egg whites until stiff peaks form. Set aside. Combine dry ingredients in separate bowl. In mixing bowl, beat coconut oil and egg yolks. Add chocolate mixture and vanilla. Beat on low until combined. Scraping down bowl to make sure well blended. Add dry ingredients and milk alternating. Beat on medium speed for 2 minutes. Fold in egg whites. Pour into flour and greased 9" x 13" pan.

Bake at 350° for 28 minutes.

Top with Coconut-Pecan Frosting while cake is still warm.

Shopping List:

1. 100% Cacao Chocolate Bar
2. Eggs
3. Coconut Oil
4. Coconut Milk
5. Vanilla
6. Blanched Almond Flour
7. Coconut Flour
8. Xanthan Gum
9. Baking Soda
10. Salt

Shopping List:

1. Coconut Milk
2. Honey
3. Coconut Oil
4. Vanilla
5. Unsweetened Coconut Flakes
6. Pecans
7. Eggs

Coconut-Pecan Frosting

¾ cup coconut milk
¼ cup water
½ cup honey
½ cup coconut oil
1 tsp. vanilla
1 ⅓ cups unsweetened coconut flakes
1 cup chopped pecans
3 egg yolks; lightly beaten

Combine milk, honey, egg yolks, coconut oil, and vanilla in saucepan. Cook and stir over medium heat until thickened. Stir in coconut flakes and pecans. Stir until spreading consistency, but it will still be a little runny while warm. Frosting will soak into cake.

Happy Easter! Why am I wishing you a Happy Easter? Because this cake goes with Easter at our house. What makes it special is we bake it in a lamb shaped pan that my mother passed down to me. I bake the cake and my children decorate it. We eat the cake early Easter morning as part of a light breakfast. I thought I was going to have to give up this tradition! Necessity breeds invention, right? I was pretty determined not to give up this fun tradition. This cake is a result of being super stubborn... some people might call that tenacity.

Shopping List:

1. Blanched Almond Flour
2. Baking Powder
3. Xanthan Gum
4. Salt
5. Unsalted Butter
6. Eggs
7. Honey
8. Vanilla

Pound Cake

Dry Ingredients:
2 ½ cups blanched almond flour
1 tsp. baking powder
1 tsp. xanthan gum
¼ tsp. salt

Combine dry ingredients in a bowl. Set aside.

Wet Ingredients:
1 ¼ cups unsalted butter
5 eggs, must be at room temperature
⅓ cup honey
2 tsp. vanilla

In mixing bowl, beat butter until fluffy. Add honey. Mix. Add eggs 1 at a time beating after each one. Scrape down bowl often. Add dry ingredients a little at a time. Beating after each addition. Add vanilla. Scrape down bowl, mix one last time.

Prepare glass loaf pan by greasing or buttering sides and bottom of pan. Lightly dust with almond flour. Pour cake batter into prepared pan. Bake at 315° for around 45 minutes. The cake should be set but do not let it dry out. You may need to bake it for more or less time depending on your oven. Let cool. Remove from pan while the cake is still warm.

To bake in lamb shaped pan: grease with vegetable shortening or butter both the top and bottom halves of pan. Lightly dust with almond flour. Make sure you do a good job or your caked won't come out of the pan! Pour cake batter into the bottom half (my top half has a little hole in it). Place top half on. Put on cookie sheet for stability. Bake at 315° for 35 minutes. Let cake cool. Remove from pan while the cake is still warm.

We frost it with a light layer of the cream cheese frosting **(see Carrot Cake recipe)** then cover it in flaked coconut for the "wool". Jelly bean or chocolate chips make the eyes and nose. We surround it with "green grass" made of flaked coconut.

To make the green grass: mix a couple of drops of green food coloring into 1 Tbsp. water, add coconut, and stir. Easy, peasy!

Strawberry Torte Cake

Dry Ingredients:
2 ⅓ cups blanched almond flour
2 tsp. baking soda
¼ tsp. salt
1 tsp. xanthan gum
⅓ cup coconut flour

Wet Ingredients:
1 cup butter; softened
3 eggs
2 tsp. vanilla
2 cups milk
10 oz. strawberry jelly (all fruit variety)

Cream butter, beat in eggs and vanilla. Mix dry ingredients in separate bowl. Alternating, add dry ingredients and milk to butter mixture Then, beat on high for 3 minutes, scraping bowl. Spread into three 8" greased and floured pans. Bake at 325° for 24-27 minutes. Spread each layer with jelly while warm, dividing the jar into 3 parts (approximately 3 ⅓ oz. each), use all of the jelly. Let cool.

Strawberry Torte Filling:
2 cups whipped cream
3 cups sliced strawberries

Assembling cake: Place one cake on serving platter with jelly side up. Layer strawberries on cake. Spread whipped cream on strawberries. Place second cake on whipped cream with jelly side up. Repeat layering strawberries and whipped cream. Place **third cake with jelly-side down** on top of whipped cream. Garnish top of cake with dollop of whipped cream and strawberries.

Shopping List:
1. Blanched Almond Flour
2. Baking Soda
3. Salt
4. Xanthan Gum
5. Coconut Flour
6. Butter
7. Vanilla
8. Eggs
9. Milk
10. Strawberry Jelly
11. Whipped Cream
12. Sliced Strawberries

Carrot Cake

Dry Ingredients:
1 cup almonds
½ cup pecans
½ cup walnuts
1 tsp. baking soda
1 tsp. baking powder
¼ tsp. salt
1 ½ tsp. cinnamon
½ tsp. ginger

Wet Ingredients:
1 cup sweet potato puree
4 eggs
½ cup unsalted butter; softened
3 cups shredded carrots (choose good, fresh carrots: your cake will taste better)

Process the almonds, pecans and walnuts together in food processor until it creates a flour mixture. Then, mix in the remaining dry ingredients and process together. Set aside. In mixing bowl, cream the butter. Add the sweet potato puree and eggs. Beat until combined, scraping down the bowl. Add dry ingredients. Beat 2 minutes, scraping down the bowl. Add shredded carrots. Mix until just combined. Pour into greased and floured 9" x 13" pan. Bake 350° for 30 minutes.

Top with cream cheese frosting after cake is cooled. Store in the refrigerator.

Cream Cheese Frosting

8 oz. cream cheese, softened
½ cup butter, softened
2 tsp. vanilla
1 Tbsp. honey; heaping

Beat together cream cheese and butter in mixing bowl. Add vanilla and honey. Beat for 1 minute more, scraping down the bowl. Frosting should be well blended and slightly fluffy. This recipe will frost a 9" x 13" cake generously.

Shopping List:

1. Blanched Almond Flour
2. Baking Soda
3. Salt
4. Xanthan Gum
5. Coconut Flour
6. Butter
7. Vanilla
8. Eggs
9. Milk
10. Strawberry Jelly
11. Whipped Cream
12. Sliced Strawberries

Shopping List:

1. Cream Cheese
2. Butter
3. Vanilla
4. Honey

Frosting

These recipes can be used with any of the cakes or cookies recipes. Sometimes it is all in the frosting...

Chocolate Buttercream Frosting

2.5 oz. unsweetened 100% chocolate cacao premium baking bar
½ cup butter
2 Tbsp. coconut oil

Melt chocolate, coconut oil, and butter together in saucepan on low heat. Let cool.

¾ cup sweet potato puree
2 tsp. vanilla
pinch of sea salt (fine)
¼ cup cocoa powder

In mixing bowl, combine sweet potato puree, cocoa powder, salt and vanilla. Slowly add chocolate mixture. Beat until combined about 1 minute, scraping bowl.

A tasty dairy-free frosting... it just doesn't get better than this!

Shopping List:

1. 100% Cacao Chocolate Bar
2. Butter
3. Coconut Oil
4. Sweet Potato Puree
5. Vanilla
6. Sea Salt
7. Cocoa Powder

Dairy-Free Chocolate Fudge Frosting

1 ¾ cups almond milk
28 prunes
8 oz. 100% cacao chocolate, premium baking bar
2 tsp. vanilla
dash of sea salt
¼ cup Earth Balance

Shopping List:

1. Almond Milk
2. Prunes
3. 100% Cacao Chocolate Bar
4. Vanilla
5. Sea Salt
6. Earth Balance

In saucepan, combine almond milk, Earth Balance, and prunes. Heat on low until prunes soften, about 5 minutes. Using a cover on the pan will soften prunes faster. Remove from heat. Add chocolate, stir. Place in food processor. Add vanilla and salt. Process until prunes are smooth and all ingredients are combined. Use while warm. Makes enough to cover a 9" X 13" pan.

You can substitute regular butter and milk for the almond milk and Earth Balance. You will end up with a really great frosting this way too.

Chocolate Butter Frosting

$1/3$ cup butter or Earth Balance (butter substitute)
½ cup cocoa powder
$1/8$ cup milk or almond milk
1 ½ tsp. vanilla
1 Tbsp. honey
Dash of salt

Combine ingredients in mixing bowl. Beat until combined. Makes enough to frost a small cake or about 6 cupcakes lightly frosted.

Shopping List:

1. Butter or Earth Balance
2. Cocoa Powder
3. Milk or Almond Milk
4. Vanilla
5. Honey
6. Salt

Candy

Chocolate Cherry Walnut Fudge

1 ¼ cups pureed cherries
6 oz. 100% chocolate premium baking bar, chopped
4 Tbsp. unsalted butter
2 Tbsp. heavy whipping cream
3 Tbsp. honey, optional (you may want to start with a sweeter fudge, then slowly decrease honey)

In a medium saucepan, combine cherries, chocolate, butter, and cream. Heat on low until chocolate is melted. Stir constantly to prevent scorching.

½ tsp. vanilla
Pinch of salt

Add vanilla and salt to chocolate mixture. Stir.

1 ¼ cups walnuts, chopped
1 ½ cups cherries, chopped

Add walnuts and cherries to chocolate mixture. Stir just until combined. Butter sides and bottom of 7" x 11" pan. Pour fudge into pan. Spread evenly. Refrigerate. Cut into squares. Store in refrigerator to stay firm. The fudge will last 2 weeks refrigerated in an air-tight container.

Shopping List:

1. 100% Cacao Chocolate Bar
2. Pureed Cherries
3. Unsalted Butter
4. Heaving Whipping Cream
5. Honey
6. Vanilla
7. Salt
8. Walnuts
9. Cherries

Honey Peanut Crunchers

1 cup honey

In medium saucepan, bring honey to boil then turn down to medium heat. Stir until you can see the bottom of the pan.

2 cups roasted peanuts
¼ tsp. vanilla
½ tsp. cinnamon

Add peanuts, cinnamon, and vanilla. Cook on medium heat 2 minutes more. Spoon into buttered mini-muffin pan. After candy has cooled, transfer to buttered candy cups.

Sea salt to dust candies with

Dust candies lightly with sea salt. Store in airtight container for up to 2 weeks.

Shopping List:

1. Honey
2. Roasted Peanuts
3. Vanilla
4. Cinnamon

Dairy-Free Mint Fudge

¼ cup cocoa powder
4 oz. 100% chocolate premium baking bar, chopped (unsweetened)
2 Tbsp. Earth Balance
2 Tbsp. honey
3 Tbsp. almond milk or coconut milk

Combine ingredients in saucepan. Cook on low heat until chocolate is melted. Stir constantly.

1 tsp. vanilla
1 ½ tsp. peppermint extract
Pinch of salt

Add vanilla, peppermint, and salt. Stir until combined. Pour into an Earth Balance "buttered" dish. Spread fudge into pan. Refrigerate until firm. Cut into squares. Will last 2 weeks refrigerated in airtight container.

> **Tip:** You may use butter and regular milk instead of the Earth Balance and almond milk. This recipe will still turn out wonderfully.

Shopping List:

1. 100% Cacao Chocolate Bar
2. Cocoa Powder
3. Earth Balance
4. Honey
5. Almond or Coconut Milk
6. Vanilla
7. Peppermint Extract
8. Salt

The next two recipes are converts from old family favorites. I make this candy at Christmas and I wanted to be able to eat it too! Instead of whining, I went to work and came up with something that is pretty tasty. The best part is I got to eat some candy and didn't put on the usual 5 extra pounds that come with the holiday. Hears to having your candy and eating it too!

Shopping List:

1. 100% Cacao Chocolate Bar
2. Cream Cheese
3. Honey
4. Instant Coffee
5. Vanilla

Mocha Truffles

Filling for Centers:
2 oz. cream cheese, softened
4 oz. 100% chocolate, chopped and melted (see below for tip on melting)
3 Tbsp. honey

Place cream cheese in small bowl. Using wooden spoon stir until soft and lump-free. Add the honey and chocolate. Stir until combined and smooth. Use electric mixture if you need to.

1 Tbsp. instant coffee
1 tsp. water
¼ tsp. vanilla

Mix together in small cup. Add to cream cheese mixture. Stir until well blended. Put into refrigerator until almost firm. Roll into small balls (1/2" in diameter). These are very rich, extreme dark chocolate flavor. You just need a little truffle to be satisfied. Put balls onto plate. Refrigerate until firm and you are ready to dip them in chocolate or roll in toppings.

Shopping List:

1. Premium Chocolate Baking Bar
   or
1. Cocoa Powder
2. Almonds

Chocolate for Dipping Centers:
Melted 70, 90, or 100% chocolate premium baking bar for dipping centers
    or
1 Tbsp. cocoa powder for rolling centers in
¼ cup almonds blended until very fine for rolling centers in

> **Tip:** Melt chocolate in "simple" double boiler. Place small heat proof bowl in saucepan. Add water to reach up side of bowl. Do not overfill water. You do not want even a drop of water to get into your chocolate. Turn on heat to low.

Simmer chocolate in double-boiler until chocolate is melted. Stirring often. Remove bowl to use chocolate. Holding centers on fork or spoon, dip into melted chocolate. Place on plate to cool and harden. You may choose to roll centers in cocoa, almonds, or leave them plain so you have variety. Store in airtight container. Refrigerating will make your candies last longer, but the chocolate may bloom (get white spots on it). If it blooms, it is still safe to eat but the candies do not look as nice. Just eat them right away and you don't have to worry about storage!

Makes about 24 truffles

Peanut Butter Balls

Filling for Centers:
½ cup unsweetened peanut butter
3 Tbsp. blanched almond flour
3 Tbsp. honey
2 Tbsp. butter, softened
Dash of sea salt

Combine peanut butter, almond flour, honey, butter, and salt in bowl. Stir until smooth. Use electric mixer if necessary. Refrigerate until firm. Roll into ball about 1" in diameter. You can make them smaller if you wish. Put balls on plate and put into refrigerator until firm and you are ready to dip them.

Chocolate for Dipping Centers:
2 oz. either 70, 90, or 100% chocolate premium baking bar

> **Tip:** Melt chocolate in "simple" double boiler. Place small heat proof bowl in saucepan. Add water to reach up side of bowl. Do not overfill water. You do not want even a drop of water to get into your chocolate. Turn on heat to low.

Simmer chocolate in double-boiler until chocolate is melted. Stirring often. Remove bowl to use chocolate. Holding centers on fork or spoon, dip into melted chocolate. Place on plate to cool and harden. Store in airtight container. Refrigerating will make your candies last longer, but the chocolate may bloom (get white spots on it). If it blooms, it is still safe to eat but the candies do not look as nice.

Makes about 18-24 candies.

Shopping List:
1. Unsweetened Peanut Butter
2. Blanched Almond Flour
3. Honey
4. Butter
5. Sea Salt
6. 100% Chocolate Baking Bar

Cookies

Pecan-Oatmeal Chocolate Chip Cookies

Dry Ingredients:

1 cup blanched almond flour
1 Tbsp. coconut flour
1/8 tsp. sea salt
¼ tsp. baking soda
1/8 tsp. xanthan gum

Combine ingredients in bowl. Set aside.

Wet Ingredients:

5 Tbsp. unsalted butter; softened some
4 Tbsp. honey
1 tsp. vanilla
1 egg

Beat in mixing bowl until combined. Scraping down bowl. Add dry ingredients. Mix until combined.

¼ cup chopped pecans
¼ cup finely chopped 100% chocolate premium baking bar
1/3 cup oatmeal

Add the pecans, chocolate, and oatmeal to dough. Mix just until combined. Place by tablespoons onto lined cookie sheet. Bake at 375° for 10 minutes.

> **Tip:** The fast method involves using a food processor. Put the dry ingredients in processor. Give it a "whir." Add the wet ingredients. Process again to blend. Last add the oatmeal, pecans, and chocolate. Process just until blended. Wa-la! Cookie dough in minutes.

Shopping List:

1. Blanched Almond Flour
2. Coconut Flour
3. Sea Salt
4. Baking Soda
5. Xanthan Gum
6. Unsalted Butter
7. Honey
8. Vanilla
9. Egg
10. Pecans
11. 100% Chocolate Baking Bar
12. Oatmeal

Pecan-Oat Raw Cookies

2 cups pecans
3 Tbsp. salted butter
1 ½ Tbsp. chia seeds
½ cup chopped raisins
¼ tsp. salt
1 ½ Tbsp. oat bran
¼ tsp. vanilla
Additional oat bran for rolling cookies in

Place pecans in food processor. Process until fine. Add butter. Blend until mixed. Add chia seeds, raisins, salt, oat bran and vanilla. Blend until forms a ball. Form into 1 ½" balls. Roll balls in oat bran. Refrigerate or freeze.

Shopping List:

1. Pecans
2. Salted Butter
3. Chia Seeds
4. Raisins
5. Salt
6. Oat Bran
7. Vanilla

Raspberry Thumbprints

¼ tsp. baking soda
1 ¼ cups gluten-free flour mix
½ tsp. xanthan gum

In small bowl, combine baking soda, flour, xanthan gum. Set aside.

4 oz. cream cheese
6 Tbsp. salted butter
2 tsp. honey
½ tsp. almond extract
½ tsp. vanilla

Place cream cheese and butter in mixing bowl. Beat until combined. Add honey, almond extract, and vanilla. Mix until combined, scraping down the bowl. Add flour mixture. Beat for 1 minute, scraping down the bowl.

Raspberry jelly (pure fruit)

Form into balls, place on parchment lined cookie sheet. Flatten. Press thumbprint into cookie but do not go all the way to the sheet. Fill with jelly. Do not overfilled thumbprint with jelly.

Bake at 325° for 13 minutes.

Shopping List:

1. Baking Soda
2. Gluten-Free Flour Mix
3. Xanthan Gum
4. Cream Cheese
5. Salted Butter
6. Honey
7. Almond Extract
8. Vanilla
9. Raspberry Jelly

Chocolate Nibblers

2 heaping cups whole almonds
4 Tbsp. Earth Balance
½ tsp. salt
2 Tbsp. chia seeds
½ cup chopped raisins
2 oz. chopped 100% chocolate premium baking bar
1 Tbsp. honey

First, process the whole almonds until it creates a butter like consistency. This should take about 5 minutes. Add the butter and salt and process it again until it creates clumps. Then, add the chia seeds and chopped raisins and process all of the ingredients again. After that, add the chocolate and honey. Blend until all ingredients are combined. Shapes into balls about 1-1 ½" in diameter. Store in refrigerator or freezer.

You can substitute regular unsalted butter for the Earth Balance.

Shopping List:

1. Almonds
2. Earth Balance
3. Salt
4. Chia Seeds
5. Chopped Raisins
6. 100% Chocolate Baking Bar
7. Honey

P.B. & J Cookies

1 cup natural peanut butter
2 medium eggs, lightly beaten
1 tsp. vanilla
⅓ cup raspberry jelly
Sea salt (optional)

First, lightly beat the eggs. Next, combine the peanut butter, eggs, and half of the jelly; save the other half of the jelly for the top of the cookies. Form balls with the dough and put on a parchment-lined cookie sheet. Flatten the balls slightly. Then, put the jelly on the tops of the cookie. You can make a thumbprint in each cookie and fill with jelly. Jelly will melt and run, so do not overfill. Dust very lightly with sea salt.

Bake at 350° for 9 minutes.

Shopping List:

1. Natural Peanut Butter
2. Eggs
3. Vanilla
4. Raspberry Jelly
5. Sea Salt

Almond Cookies (Bird Seed Cookies)

2 cups almonds (whole) or almond flour
¼ cup ground flax seed
½ tsp. baking soda
¼ tsp. fine sea salt
2 Tbsp. coconut oil
1 tsp. vanilla
1 tsp. almond extract
1 Tbsp. almond milk
½ cup sliced almonds
1 egg

First, grind the whole almonds in a food processor until it reaches it fine texture. Then, add the remaining ingredients, excluding the sliced almonds, and blend until they are equally combined. After that, add the sliced almonds and pulse until it is just blended; do not over process. Then, place, on a parchment-lined cookie sheet, by heaping teaspoons. Afterwards, flatten into 2" diameter circles. Finally, bake at 350° for 8 minutes.

Shopping List:

1. Almonds or Almond Flour
2. Ground Flax Seed
3. Baking Soda
4. Fine Sea Salt
5. Coconut Oil
6. Vanilla
7. Almond Extract
8. Almond Milk
9. Sliced Almonds
10. Egg

"Sugar" Cookies

Dry Ingredients:
2 ½ cups almond flour
½ cup coconut flour
½ tsp. baking soda
pinch salt
1 tsp. xanthan gum

In a small bowl, combine almond flour, coconut flour, baking soda, salt, and xanthan gum. Set aside.

Wet Ingredients:
½ cup softened butter
3 oz. cream cheese- softened
2 eggs
2 ½ tsp. vanilla
1 Tbsp. honey (heaping)

Beat the butter and cream cheese together. Add eggs. Mix until combined, scraping down the bowl. Add vanilla and honey. Mix until well blended. Add flour mixture and mix until combined. Scooping into tablespoon size amount, place on parchment lined cookie sheets. Flatten slightly with the bottom of a glass.

Bake at 350° for 8 minutes.

Shopping List:
1. Blanched Almond Flour
2. Coconut Flour
3. Baking Soda
4. Salt
5. Xanthan Gum
6. Butter
7. Cream Cheese
8. Eggs
9. Vanilla
10. Honey

Fruit Pizza

1 batch sugar cookies
8 oz. cream cheese, softened
Honey, to taste
Blueberries
Oranges
Raspberries
Strawberries
Kiwi

Mix honey and cream cheese. Frost cookies with cream cheese mixture. Arrange fruit on top of cookie. Enjoy!

Shopping List:

1. Blanched Almond Flour
2. Coconut Flour
3. Baking Soda
4. Salt
5. Xanthan Gum
6. Butter
7. Cream Cheese
8. Eggs
9. Vanilla
10. Honey
11. Blueberries
12. Oranges
13. Raspberries
14. Strawberries
15. Kiwi

Chocolate Chip Cookies

Wet Ingredients:
1 cup blanched almond flour
1 Tbsp. coconut flour
⅛ tsp. sea salt
¼ tsp. baking soda
⅛ tsp. xanthan gum

In a small bowl, combine almond flour, coconut flour, oatmeal, salt, baking soda, and xanthan gum. Set aside.

Dry Ingredients:
5 Tbsp. unsalted butter
4 Tbsp. honey
1 tsp. Vanilla
1 egg

In a mixing bowl, beat the butter, honey, vanilla, and egg. Scrape down bowl and add the flour mixture. Mix until combined.

¼ cup chopped 100% chocolate

Add the chocolate to dough. Mix until just combined. Place on parchment-lined cookie sheet. Flatten cookies.

Bake at 350° for 8 minutes.

Shopping List:
1. Blanched Almond Flour
2. Coconut Flour
3. Sea Salt
4. Baking Soda
5. Xanthan Gum
6. Unsalted Butter
7. Honey
8. Vanilla
9. Egg

Gingerbread Cookies

Dry Ingredients:
3 ½ cups blanched almond flour
2 Tbsp. coconut flour
1 tsp. baking soda
1 tsp. cinnamon
1 tsp. ginger
¼ tsp. ground cloves
½ tsp. salt
1 tsp. xanthan gum

In a small bowl, combine above ingredients. Set aside.

Wet Ingredients:
½ cup softened butter
½ cup molasses
$^1/_3$ cup water

Beat the butter and molasses together. Mix until combined, scraping down the bowl. Add flour mixture and mix until combined. Adding water a little at a time. Roll out dough to ¼" thick. Using cookie cutters cut out shapes. Carefully place cookies on parchment lined baking sheet.

Bake at 350° for 10 minutes.

Shopping List:

1. Blanched Almond Flour
2. Coconut Flour
3. Sea Salt
4. Baking Soda
5. Xanthan Gum
6. Cinnamon
7. Ginger
8. Ground Cloves
9. Butter
10. Molasses

Desserts

Chocolate Coconut Mousse

3 Tbsp. butter
1 Tbsp. coconut oil
1 Tbsp. vanilla
2 heaping Tbsp. cocoa powder

Melt butter on very low heat. Remove from heat. Add coconut oil, vanilla, and cocoa. Cool.

1 pint whipping cream
Flaked unsweetened coconut (optional)

Whip cream until soft peaks form. Add the chocolate mix. Whip just until combined. Garnish with flaked coconut.

Shopping List:

1. Butter
2. Coconut Oil
3. Vanilla
4. Cocoa Powder
5. Whipping Cream
6. Flaked Unsweetened Coconut

Lemon Lime Curd

3 ½ Tbsp. corn starch
½ cup honey
1 ½ cups water

Combine cornstarch, honey, and water. Cook until thickened

3 egg yolks, beaten in large heat-proof bowl (glass)

Gradually add the cornstarch mixture to the beaten egg yolks, whisking while pouring the cornstarch mixture into the egg yolks. The stream of liquid should be very small… you don't want to add it too quickly or it will scramble your eggs! Now that wouldn't make for a very appetizing dessert at all. Bring mixture to a gentle simmer. Cook 2 minutes. Stirring constantly.

2 Tbsp. butter (Earth Balance for dairy-free)
1 tsp. lemon zest
1 tsp. lime zest

Stir in butter, lemon, and lime peel.

¼ cup lemon juice (juice of 1 lemon)
3 Tbsp. lime juice (juice of 1 lime)
Pinch of salt

Gradually add juice and salt. Stir gently. Pour into dessert dishes.

Variation:
Add raspberry jelly to lemon-lime curd

¾ cup curd to 1 heaping tsp. Jelly

Add while warm. Whisk.

Shopping List:

1. Corn Starch
2. Honey
3. Egg
4. Lemon Zest
5. Lime Zest
6. Salt
7. Raspberry Jelly (OPTIONAL)

Fudge Brownies

½ cup butter
2 oz. unsweetened chocolate (100% premium baking bar), melted

Melt butter and chocolate over very low heat. Stirring constantly. Remove from heat and set aside.

½ cup prunes
¼ cup water

Combine prunes and water in saucepan and cook until prunes are soft. Add more water if needed. Using a cover will decrease cooking time. Cool slightly and puree.

½ cup sweet potatoes
¾ cup ground almonds
2 eggs
1 tsp. vanilla

Add sweet potatoes, ground almonds, eggs, and vanilla to prune puree. Blend. Add chocolate mixture and blend.

1 cup chopped walnuts

Add walnuts to food processor and blend just till combined. Place in a greased 7" x 11" baking dish. Double batch fills a 9" x 13" pan.

Bake at 350° for 23 minutes for single batch, about 45 minutes for double batch.

Fudge Brownie Frosting

1 cup cream
14 prunes
4 oz. unsweetened chocolate (100% premium baking bar), chopped

Combine cream and prunes in saucepan. Heat on very low heat until prunes are softened. Covering the pan will shortened cooking time. Add chocolate. Stir until melted. Puree in food processor.

Shopping List:

1. Butter
2. 100% Chocolate Baking Bar
3. Prunes
4. Sweet Potatoes
5. Ground Almonds
6. Eggs
7. Vanilla
8. Walnuts

Shopping List:

1. Cream
2. Prunes
3. 100% Chocolate Baking Bar
4. Salt
5. Vanilla

1 tsp. Vanilla
Dash of sea salt

Add vanilla and sea salt to chocolate mixture. Blend. Spread on brownies while warm. This may make extra frosting depending on how thick you want your frosting on the brownies. Store any extra frosting in fridge.

Chocolate Pudding

½ cup cocoa powder
⅓-½ cup honey
2 Tbsp. corn starch
⅛ tsp. salt
3½ cups milk
2 beaten eggs

In a saucepan, combine cocoa, honey cornstarch, salt. Add milk. Whisk to combine and cook over medium heat until mixture comes to a simmer. Cook 2 minutes, stirring constantly. It will begin to thicken. Gradually add the chocolate mixture to the beaten egg yolks, whisking while pouring the chocolate mixture into the egg yolks. The stream of liquid should be very small… you don't want to add it too quickly or it will scramble your eggs!   Return chocolate mixture to pan and cook on low heat for 2 minutes. Stirring constantly. Remove from heat

1 Tbsp. butter
1½ tsp vanilla

Add the butter and vanilla to pudding. Stir until combined. Pour into dessert dishes and let set. You may serve this pudding warm with a scoop of vanilla ice-cream or cold as a parfait with berries and whipped cream. You can make it as fancy or simple as you wish. Either way it will be a favorite with your family and friends.

You can substitute rice or almond milk for the cow's milk and Earth Balance for the butter for a great dairy-free dessert. I prefer the rice milk over the almond milk… just my personal taste. I have made it all three ways (cow's milk, rice milk, and almond milk) and everyone who tastes it, loves it, regardless of the milk used.

Shopping List:

1. Cocoa Powder
2. Honey
3. Corn Starch
4. Salt
5. Milk
6. Eggs
7. Butter
8. Vanilla

Vanilla Pudding

⅓-½ cup honey
3 Tbsp. corn starch
⅛ tsp. salt
3½ cups milk
2 beaten eggs

In a saucepan, combine honey, cornstarch, salt. Add milk. Whisk to combine and cook over medium heat until mixture comes to a simmer. Cook 2 minutes, stirring constantly. It will begin to thicken. Gradually add the mixture to the beaten egg yolks, whisking while pouring the mixture into the egg yolks. The stream of liquid should be very small… you don't want to add it too quickly or it will scramble your eggs!   Return mixture to pan and cook on low heat for 2 minutes. Stirring constantly. Remove from heat

1 Tbsp. butter
2 Tbsp. vanilla

Add the butter and vanilla to pudding. Stir until combined. Pour into dessert dishes and let set. Refrigerate if not serving warm.

Shopping List:

1. Honey
2. Corn Starch
3. Salt
4. Milk
5. Eggs
6. Butter
7. Vanilla

Ice Cream

When trying to eat for healthy living, I have to admit; I missed ice-cream! I missed it so much that it was often my weak point every summer. Just like that, I would be back on the crazy cycle of eating too much junk! I finally came to my senses and started making some delicious ice-cream that satisfied my need for a cool treat on a hot summer day. My daughter and I had a great summer coming up with new recipes and of course taste testing them too!

Some of the recipes are sweeter than others. When you are making the switch to healthy eating, you may want to start with: Banana, or the Pineapple-Mango ice-cream. You can also add ¼ to ½ cup warmed honey to the milk in order to sweeten any of the recipes. If you like chocolate, you can make the hot fudge sauce to put over any of the ice-creams. Lots of options for making the switch!

Tip: Homemade ice-cream is much harder than purchased ice-cream. I have found two ways around this.

Method One: Down and Dirty...Give me my Ice-cream! Follow directions for recipe and pour into paper cups after churning ice-cream. Cover with aluminum foil and freeze. Take out of freezer 10 minutes before you want to eat it.

Method Two: I have some self-control and don't mind washing an extra bowl. Instead of pouring the cream into ice-cream maker to churn with the rest of the ingredients, whip it in a mixing bowl until stiff peaks forms. Fold whipped cream into the churned ice-cream. Freeze.

Either way works! Method two is closer to purchased ice-cream and it is easier to scoop from a large container.

Peach Ice Cream

2 peaches; pureed (1 ¼ cups)
2 cups whole milk
2 cups heavy whipping cream
2 Tbsp. Mexican vanilla (can substitute regular vanilla)
1 cup pear puree

In a large bowl, add pureed peaches, milk, heavy whipping cream, Mexican vanilla and pear puree. Stir. Pour into ice-cream maker and follow manufacturer's directions. After ice-cream is done churning, pour ice-cream into a freezer container.

3 cups chopped peaches
⅛ tsp. sea salt

Add the chopped peaches and sea salt. Fold ingredients together until combined. Freeze.

Shopping List:

1. Pureed Peaches
2. Whole Milk
3. Heavy Whipping Cream
4. Vanilla
5. Pear Puree
6. Chopped Peaches
7. Sea Salt

Chocolate Almond Dairy-Free Ice Cream

2 cups almond milk
6 oz. chopped 70% chocolate premium baking bar

Simmer the almond milk. Add chocolate. Stir. Set aside.

16 prunes
13.5 oz. can of coconut milk; unsweetened
¼ cup Earth Balance
1 Tbsp. vanilla; Penzey's single strength

Combine the prunes, coconut milk, and Earth Balance. Cook on low until the prunes have softened. Puree until smooth. Add vanilla and the chocolate mixture. Puree again. Pour into ice-cream maker and follow manufacturer's directions.

2 cups sliced almonds

Stir in sliced almonds after churning. Pour into paper cups or freezer safe container. Freeze.

This is a very good recipe to start with when changing how you eat your treats. This one hasn't failed me yet. Even die-hard sugar hounds like it. Remember to chop the chocolate finely or it will make the ice-cream taste too bitter.

Shopping List:

1. Almond Milk
2. 70% Chocolate Baking Bar
3. Prunes
4. Unsweetened Coconut Milk
5. Earth Balance
6. Vanilla
7. Sliced Almonds

Mint-Chocolate Chip Ice Cream

1 ½ cups pears; pureed (about 4 pears)
2 cups whole milk
2 cups heavy whipping cream
1 ½ Tbsp. peppermint extract
1 Tbsp. vanilla
A few drops Green food coloring, optional

In a large bowl, add pureed pears, milk, heavy whipping cream, vanilla, food coloring, and mint extract. Stir. Pour into ice-cream maker and follow manufacturer's directions. After ice-cream is done churning, pour ice-cream into a freezer container.

4 oz. finely chopped 100% cacao chocolate premium baking bar

Add the chopped chocolate. Fold ingredients together until combined. Freeze.

Shopping List:

1. Pureed Pears
2. Whole Milk
3. Heavy Whipping Cream
4. Peppermint Extract
5. Vanilla
6. Green Food Coloring (optional)
7. 100% Chocolate Baking Bar

Vanilla Ice Cream

2 cups whole milk
1 ¾ cups pear puree
2 cups heavy whipping cream
2 Tbsp. Mexican vanilla

Mix ingredients together in a bowl. Pour into ice-cream maker and follow manufacturer's directions. After ice-cream is done churning, pour ice-cream into a freezer container. Freeze.

Variation:
In order to get the black flecks of color in your vanilla ice-cream, you need vanilla beans. I thought it would impart more vanilla flavor as well. The jury is still out on that. Give it a try.... Everyone's taste buds are different.

2 vanilla beans
2 cups whole milk

Gently simmer vanilla beans in milk. When beans are soft, remove from heat. With a knife, slice open the vanilla bean and scrape the black, vanilla bean insides. You will see tiny black, individual seeds. Put the scrapings from both beans into the milk and stir. Discard the vanilla bean pods. Cool the vanilla milk mixture in the refrigerator. This will make churning process faster.

1 ¾ cups pear puree
2 cups heavy whipping cream
2 Tbsp. Mexican vanilla extract

Combine the vanilla milk with the pear puree, whipping cream and the vanilla extract. Pour into ice-cream maker and follow manufacturer's directions. After ice-cream is done churning, pour ice-cream into a freezer container. Freeze.

Shopping List:

1. Whole Milk
2. Pear Puree
3. Heavy Whipping Cream
4. Vanilla
5. Vanilla Beans (optional)

Banana Fudge Swirl

6 bananas, pureed (3 cups)
2 Tbsp. vanilla
2 cups whole milk
2 cups heavy whipping cream

Combine the banana puree, milk, whipping cream and the vanilla extract. Pour into ice-cream maker and follow manufacturer's directions. Make the fudge while the ice-cream is churning. Spread fudge on inside of freezer container, reserve some fudge to swirl into ice-cream.

After ice-cream is done churning, pour ice-cream into a freezer container. "Swirl" remaining fudge into ice-cream. It feels more like laying strips of fudge into the ice-cream than swirling! Put in freezer.

Shopping List:

1. Bananas
2. Vanilla
3. Whole Milk
4. Heavy Whipping Cream

Fudge

1 cup heavy whipping cream; warmed
14 prunes

Put cream in saucepan. Heat over very low heat. Do not allow to boil. Add the prunes to the warm cream. Cover. Let the prunes soften.

4 oz. 100% unsweetened cacao chocolate premium baking bar, chopped
1 tsp. vanilla
dash of sea salt

Add the chocolate, salt, and vanilla to prune mixture. Stir until chocolate is melted. Pour into blender or food processor and puree. Allow to cool.

Shopping List:

1. Heavy Whipping Cream
2. Prunes
3. 100% Chocolate Baking Bar
4. Vanilla
5. Sea Salt

Banana Ice Cream

6 bananas, pureed (3 cups)
2 Tbsp. vanilla
2 cups whole milk
2 cups heavy whipping cream

Combine the banana puree, milk, whipping cream and the vanilla extract. Pour into ice-cream maker and follow manufacturer's directions. After ice-cream is done churning, pour ice-cream into a freezer container. Freeze.

Optional:
For more banana flavor, add 3 bananas, chopped (1 ½ cups) to churned ice-cream. Freeze.

Shopping List:

1. Pureed Bananas
2. Vanilla
3. Whole Milk
4. Heavy Whipping Cream

Strawberry Ice Cream

4 cups pureed strawberries
2 Tbsp. vanilla
2 cups whole milk
2 cups heavy whipping cream
½ cup pear puree

Combine the strawberry and pear puree, milk, whipping cream and the vanilla extract. Pour into ice-cream maker and follow manufacturer's directions. After ice-cream is done churning, pour ice-cream into a freezer container. Freeze.

Optional:
For more strawberry flavor, add 1 ½ cups chopped strawberries to churned ice-cream. Freeze.

Shopping List:

1. Pureed Strawberries
2. Vanilla
3. Whole Milk
4. Heavy Whipping Cream
5. Pear Puree
6. Strawberries

Raspberry Ice Cream

2 ½ cups raspberries

Cook raspberries in small saucepan over low heat. You may add 1 tbsp. of water to prevent scorching. Puree. You should end up with 1 ¼ cups puree. Put in refrigerator to cool.

2 Tbsp. vanilla
2 cups whole milk
2 cups heavy whipping cream
2 cups pear puree (4 pears)

Combine the raspberry puree, pear puree, milk, whipping cream and the vanilla extract. Pour into ice-cream maker and follow manufacturer's directions. After ice-cream is done churning, pour ice-cream into a freezer container.

2 cups whole raspberries

Add raspberries to churned ice-cream. Freeze.

Shopping List:

1. Raspberries
2. Vanilla
3. Whole Milk
4. Heavy Whipping Cream
5. Pear Puree

Pineapple-Orange-Mango Ice Cream

2 cups heavy whipping cream
2 cups whole milk
¾ cup frozen pineapple-orange juice; concentrate (do not mix with water)
1 Tbsp. Bourbon vanilla extract (can use plain vanilla extract)

In a large bowl, add milk, heavy whipping cream, vanilla, and juice. Stir. Pour into ice-cream maker and follow manufacturer's directions. Once churning is complete, pour into freezer container.

2 cups chopped mango (2 mangoes)
1 ½ cups chopped banana (2-3 bananas)

Mix mangoes and bananas into churned ice-cream. Freeze. Remember: you can put the churned ice-cream into paper cups too. Cover them with aluminum foil to protect the flavor and freeze.

Shopping List:

1. Heavy Whipping Cream
2. Whole Milk
3. Frozen Pineapple-Orange Juice Concentrate
4. Bourbon Vanilla Extract
5. Mango
6. Banana

Chocolate Cherry Truffle Ice Cream

¼ cup cocoa powder
6 oz. 100% unsweetened cacao chocolate premium baking bar; chopped
2 cups heavy whipping cream

Bring cream to simmer in saucepan. Add chopped chocolate. Stir until melted. Whisk in cocoa powder.

2 cups whole milk
1 cup cherry juice
1 Tbsp. vanilla

Whisk milk, juice, and vanilla into the chocolate mixture. Place in refrigerator to cool. This will speed up the churning process. Pour into ice-cream maker and follow manufacturer's directions. After ice-cream is done churning, pour ice-cream into a freezer container.

3 cups chopped cherries; Bing Cherries

Mix cherries into ice-cream. Freeze. Remember: you can pour the ice-cream into paper cups to make individual servings. Cover them with aluminum foil.

Shopping List:

1. Cocoa Powder
2. 100% Chocolate Baking Bar
3. Heavy Whipping Cream
4. Whole Milk
5. Cherry Juice
6. Vanilla
7. Cherries

Hot Fudge Sauce

4 oz. 100% chocolate premium baking bar, chopped
¼ cup butter
¼ cup honey
⅔ cup evaporated milk
Dash salt

Add all ingredients to small saucepan. Simmer gently over low heat for 6 minutes. Stirring constantly. Use fudge or pour into container and refrigerate. Will last for weeks refrigerated.

Makes: 1 ½ cups

Shopping List:

1. 100% Chocolate Baking Bar
2. Butter
3. Honey
4. Evaporated Milk
5. Salt

Chocolate Almond Ice Cream

1 ½ cups heavy whipping cream
½ cup of Half and Half

Simmer the heavy whipping cream with the half and half.

4 oz 100% unsweetened chocolate premium baking bar; chopped

Add the chopped chocolate and stir until combined. Set aside

16 prunes
2 cups whole milk

Combine the prunes and milk in saucepan. Heat on very low heat until the prunes are soft. Puree.

1 Tbsp. vanilla

Mix together the vanilla, prune mixture, and the chocolate mixture. Pour into ice-cream maker and follow manufacturer's directions.

2 cups sliced almonds

Stir in sliced almonds after churning. Pour into paper cups or freezer safe container. Freeze.

Shopping List:

1. Heavy Whipping Cream
2. Half and Half
3. 100% Chocolate Baking Bar
4. Prunes
5. Whole Milk
6. Vanilla
7. Sliced Almonds

Muffins and Scones

Apple Walnut Muffins

2 cups ground walnuts
¼ cup millet seeds
2 Tbsp. chia seeds
1 ½ tsp. baking powder
1 tsp. baking soda
¼ tsp. salt

Combine in bowl. Set aside

2 eggs
½ cup applesauce
2 tsp. vanilla
2 Tbsp. apple balsamic vinegar (or balsamic vinegar)
6 Tbsp. unsalted butter, softened

Place butter in mixing bowl. Beat until butter is fluffy. Add remain ingredients and mix until combined. Add dry ingredients. Mix just until combined. Scrape down bowl.

2 cups chopped apples
1 cup chopped walnuts

Add apples and walnuts to batter. Mix until combined. Spoon into lined muffin tin. Fill to top…this will not rise. Bake at 350° for 15 minutes or until set.

Makes 12 muffins.

Shopping List:

1. Walnuts
2. Millet Seeds
3. Chia Seeds
4. Baking Powder
5. Baking Soda
6. Salt
7. Eggs
8. Applesauce
9. Vanilla
10. Apple Balsamic Vinegar
11. Unsalted Butter
12. Apples

Pumpkin-Raisin Muffins

1 cup oatmeal
1 ½ cups ground almonds
1 ½ tsp. baking powder
1 tsp. baking soda
¼ tsp. salt
2 ½ tsp. cinnamon
1 tsp. ginger
½ tsp. cloves
¼ tsp. nutmeg

Mix all the ingredients together in bowl.

½ cup butter; unsalted softened
4 cups pumpkin puree* or canned pumpkin (room temperature)
1 cup applesauce (room temperature)
2 eggs
2 tsp. vanilla

Place butter in mixing bowl and beat for about 1 minutes or until butter is fluffy. Add pumpkin and applesauce, mix. Scrape down bowl and mix again. Add eggs and vanilla. Beat until combined. Add the dry ingredients about 1 cup at a time. Mix after each addition of dry ingredients. Scrape down bowl after mixing. Beat until just combined.

2 cups raisins
2 cups chopped pecans

Add raisins and pecans. Mix until combined.

Place batter in lined muffin tin. Fill the cups…these will not rise that much. Makes about 30 muffins.

Bake at 350° for 20 – 24 minutes.

> **Tip:** Flip back to the "Just to Make Things Easier" section to learn how to make your own pumpkin puree.

Shopping List:

1. Oatmeal
2. Almonds
3. Baking Powder
4. Baking Soda
5. Salt
6. Cinnamon
7. Ginger
8. Cloves
9. Nutmeg
10. Butter
11. Pumpkin Puree or Canned Pumpkin
12. Applesauce
13. Eggs
14. Vanilla
15. Raisins
16. Pecans

Orange-Cranberry Muffins

½ cup coconut flour
1 cup ground oatmeal
2 tsp. baking powder
½ tsp. salt
Pinch of nutmeg

Combine ingredients in a bowl, set aside.

½ Tbsp. orange zest
2 eggs lightly beaten
1 cup whole milk
2 Tbsp. orange juice; frozen, concentrate (do not mix in water)
¼ cup blood orange olive oil or canola oil

Place zest, eggs, milk, juice, and oil in a mixing bowl. Combine. Add in dry ingredients, a little at a time. Mix after each addition, scraping down the bowl at least once.

1 cup dried cranberries
½ cup chopped pecans; optional

Add cranberries and pecans to batter. Stir until combined. Place in lined muffin tin. Fill cups almost to the top.

Bake at 350° for 11 minutes for mini-muffins.

Shopping List:

1. Coconut Flour
2. Oatmeal
3. Baking Powder
4. Salt
5. Nutmeg
6. Orange Zest
7. Eggs
8. Whole Milk
9. Frozen Orange Juice Concentrate
10. Blood Orange Olive Oil or Canola Oil
11. Dried Cranberries
12. Pecans (optional)

Pecan-Apricot Scones

2 cups ground pecans
¼ cup ground flax
1 ½ tsp. baking powder
¼ tsp. salt
1 tsp. cinnamon
pinch of nutmeg

Combine ingredients in bowl and set aside.

3 Tbsp. butter; unsalted

Work the butter into dry ingredients with a fork, or place all ingredients in food processor and pulse. The mixture should be dry and crumbly looking.

2 eggs, slightly beaten
½ cup whole milk
2 tsp. vanilla

Combine eggs, milk, and vanilla. Add to the butter mixture. Stir or pulse just until combined.

1 cup chopped apricots
½ cup chopped pecans

Add apricots and pecans to mixture. Stir or pulse until combined.

For quick scones: Place batter into muffin tins. Bake at 375° for 10 minutes.

For traditional scones: Shape into a ball. Pat down into a 9" circle, ½" thick on parchment lined cookie sheet. Bake at 325° for 25 minutes. Cut into wedges. Makes 8 scones, but this depends on how big you want your pieces!

Shopping List:

1. Pecans
2. Ground Flax
3. Baking Powder
4. Salt
5. Cinnamon
6. Nutmeg
7. Unsalted Butter
8. Eggs
9. Whole Milk
10. Vanilla
11. Apricots

Oatmeal-Raisin Scones

1 cup ground almonds
1 cup oatmeal
1 tsp. baking powder
1 tsp. baking soda
1 tsp. xanthan gum
¼ tsp. salt

Combine ingredients in bowl.

½ cup unsalted butter

Cut butter into dry ingredients. Use a fork or pastry cutter to combine. Dough should be dry and crumbly.

½ cup butter milk or sour milk (½ cup milk plus 1 Tbsp. lemon juice)
1 cup raisins

Add milk to butter mixture. Stir. Blend in raisins. Knead by hand if necessary to combine. Scones are typically sort of dry. Shape into a ball. Pat down into a 9" circle, ½" thick on parchment lined cookie sheet. Bake at 325° for 25 minutes. Cut into wedges. Makes 8 scones, but this depends on how big you want your pieces!

Shopping List:

1. Almonds
2. Oatmeal
3. Baking Powder
4. Baking Soda
5. Xanthan Gum
6. Salt
7. Unsalted Butter
8. Butter Milk or Sour Milk
9. Raisins

125

Pies

Apple Galatte

1 Roll-out Pie Crust Recipe

Roll out dough into 12" circle. Grease parchment paper. Place paper on cookie sheet. Set the dough onto parchment lined sheet. Following recipe for filling.

Apple Filling:

6 cups sliced Pink Lady organic apples (approximately 6 apples)
2 tsp. cinnamon
2 tsp. lemon juice

Combine apple slices and lemon juice. Add cinnamon. Mix. Pour apple mixture into the center of the prepared crust. Fold the edges (about 3" from outer edge) over the filling for a rustic pie. Bake 325° for 25 minutes then cover loosely with aluminum foil and bake 10 minutes more.

Optional:

1-2 Tbsp. honey for a sweeter pie
2 Tbsp. water for a pie with soft, juicy apples

Mix in with sliced apples before pouring onto crust.

> **Tip:** You can use any fruit you can slice in place of the apples. Peaches or plums would make a great pie too.

Shopping List:

1. Blanched Almond Flour
2. Coconut Flour
3. Xanthan Gum
4. Baking Soda
5. Sea Salt
6. Egg
7. Butter
8. Vanilla
9. Pink Lady Apples
10. Cinnamon
11. Lemon Juice
12. Honey (optional)

Bing Cherry Pie

1 Almond Pie Crust Recipe
1 Crumb Top Recipe

Bing Cherry Pie Filling:
4 cups pitted frozen or fresh Bing Cherries
¼ cup tapioca flour (can substitute cornstarch)

Mix. Let stand 15 minutes until partially thawed if using frozen cherries. Pour cherry filling into prepared almond pie crust. Sprinkle crumb topping on cherry filling. Bake 325° for 56 minutes. Cover with aluminum foil and bake 9 minutes more.

> **Tip:** You can use any fruit that bakes well in place of the cherries. Blueberries or Raspberries would taste wonderful in this pie! You may need to add 1 Tbsp. of honey if the berries aren't sweet enough on their own.

Shopping List:

1. Almonds
2. Coconut Flour
3. Xanthan Gum
4. Unsalted Butter
5. Vanilla
6. Salt
7. Walnuts
8. Honey
9. Crumb Top Recipe
10. Bing Cherries
11. Tapioca Flour or Corn Starch

Chocolate Raspberry Cheesecake Pie

You can make the tasty pie one of two ways: the standard 9" pie that looks and tastes great cut into wedges or the individual tiny serving which is a little more labor intensive but will feed many more people. That's if they don't find the treat irresistible and forget god manners!

To make 9" Pie:
1 Chocolate Pie Crust

Bake crust at 325° for 10 minutes or until just set and firm.

Raspberry Filling:
1/4 cup raspberry jelly (100% fruit)

Stir jelly until smooth. Spread on the sides and bottom of pie crust.

Chocolate Filling:
2 oz. 100% chocolate premium baking bar, chopped
¼ cup whipping cream
1 Tbsp. raspberry jelly

Pour cream into saucepan. Warm over low heat. Do not boil. Add chocolate and raspberry jelly. Stir until chocolate is smooth. Spread on sides and bottom of pie crust.

1 cup frozen or fresh raspberries

Sprinkle raspberries over bottom of pie crust.

Cheesecake Filling:
1 egg
8 oz. cream cheese, softened
1 ½ Tbsp. lemon juice
3 tsp. vanilla
1 tbsp. honey
2 Tbsp. whole milk

Beat cream cheese until smooth. Add egg, lemon juice, vanilla, honey, and milk. Mix until fluffy and well blended. Pour into crust over raspberries. Bake pie at 325° for 15-20 minutes or until toothpick inserted in

Shopping List:
1. Almonds
2. Coconut Flour
3. Butter
4. Cocoa Powder
5. Honey
6. Xanthan Gum
7. Salt
8. Raspberry Jelly
9. 100% Chocolate Baking Bar
10. Whipping Cream
11. Raspberries
12. Egg
13. Cream Cheese
14. Lemon Juice
15. Vanilla
16. Honey
17. Whole Milk

center comes out clean. If edge of crust is getting too dark, cover with foil by cutting out a 10" circle, fold it in half and cut out the center leaving a 3" edge. Place over the edge of the crust trying not to get it stuck in the cheesecake.

To make mini pies:
1 Chocolate Pie Crust

Press crust into mini muffin pan. Make sure the bottom is thick enough and the sides are pressed in well. You may use paper liners in the muffin pan.

Raspberry Filling:
¼ cup raspberry jelly (100% fruit)

Stir jelly until smooth. Dab on the sides and bottom of mini pie crusts. Use about ¼ tsp. per mini crust.

Chocolate Filling:
2 oz. 100% chocolate premium baking bar, chopped
¼ cup whipping cream
1 Tbsp. raspberry jelly

Pour cream into saucepan. Warm over low heat. Do not boil. Add chocolate and raspberry jelly. Stir until chocolate is smooth. Spread on sides and bottom of mini pie crust. Use about ¼ tsp. per mini crust.

Cheesecake Filling:
1 egg
8 oz. cream cheese, softened
1 ½ Tbsp. lemon juice
3 tsp. vanilla
1 tbsp. honey
2 Tbsp. whole milk

Beat cream cheese until smooth. Add egg, lemon juice, vanilla, honey, and milk. Mix until fluffy and well blended. Spoon by tablespoon into mini crusts. Do not overfill.

1 cup frozen or fresh raspberries

Insert 1 whole raspberry into each mini pie being careful not to break crust. Bake mini pies at 325° for 20 minutes or until toothpick inserted in center comes out clean. Remove from muffin tin after cooled.

Pairing two great recipes together.... Lemon-Lime Pudding and Meringue Crust. I have a confession to make; when I started developing this cookbook, I had a taste for lemon meringue pie soooo I needed a flourless crust and tasty tart filling without sugar. My niece loved the filling so much that we decided to split it off into its own recipe becoming Lemon-Lime Pudding. Now you just need to put the dynamic duo back together.

Shopping List:
1. Egg
2. Cream of Tartar
3. Vanilla
4. Honey
5. Xanthan Gum
6. Corn Starch
7. Lemon Zest
8. Lime Zest
9. Salt
10. Raspberry Jelly (OPTIONAL)

Lemon-Lime Pie

Meringue Crust Recipe
Lemon-Lime Pudding Recipe for pie filling

Prepare meringue crust following recipe directions. Allow crust to cool.

Prepare lemon-lime pudding recipe as crust is baking. Stir pudding to help it cool slightly. Pour pudding into prepared crust while pudding is still warm, this will give your pie a smooth surface. Allow to cool to room temperature. Serve immediately; this pie does not store well.

Peach-Blueberry Crisp with Maple Balsamic

3 cups chopped peaches fresh or frozen
1 cup blueberries fresh or frozen
1 tsp. Mexican vanilla (can substitute regular vanilla)
1/4 tsp. cinnamon
1 Tbsp. honey (if fruit isn't sweet enough)

Mix fruit, vanilla, and cinnamon. Pout into 9" x 13" baking pan.

1 cup chopped pecans
¼ tsp. cinnamon
4 Tbsp. butter, cut into cubes
Pinch of salt

Combine ingredients. Use fingers or fork to crumble butter. Sprinkle over fruit. Bake at 350° for 30-40 minutes or until fruit is hot and bubbly.

Maple flavored balsamic vinegar for drizzling over finished crisp.

> **Tip:** For a more traditional crisp you can add 1 cup old-fashioned oatmeal to the pecan mixture.

Shopping List:

1. Peaches
2. Blueberries
3. Vanilla
4. Cinnamon
5. Honey
6. Butter
7. Salt

Crusts

Roll-out Pie Crust

Dry Ingredients:

1 ½ cups blanched almond flour
2 Tbsp. coconut flour
1 tsp. xanthan gum
¼ tsp. baking soda
1/8 tsp. sea salt

Place ingredients in bowl. Mix. Set aside.

Wet Ingredients:
1 large egg, beaten
4 Tbsp. butter
1 tsp. vanilla

Combine wet ingredients in small bowl. Add to dry flour mixture. Using a fork or pastry cutter combine into dough. You may need to work it with your hands for it to be smooth. Form into a ball. Wrap in wax paper or parchment paper and put in refrigerator to chill for 15 minutes.

Remove from fridge and roll out into a 12" circle onto greased or buttered parchment paper. You may need to dust your rolling pin with some almond flour to prevent sticking. Leave it on the parchment for a galatte. The crust is now ready for filling. See Apple Galatte filling recipe.

If you want to make a recipe with a custard type filling (chocolate for example) place the rolled-out crust into a buttered pie plate. Form the edge of the pie crust by pinching the dough between your thumb on one hand and thumb and first finger on the other. This will make a traditional "V" edge. Bake crust at 325° for 15 minutes or until crust is just turning brown and is set. Allow to cool then add filling.

Shopping List:

1. Blanched Almond Flour
2. Coconut Flour
3. Xanthan Gum
4. Baking Soda
5. Sea Salt
6. Egg
7. Butter
8. Vanilla

Almond Pie Crust

2 cups finely ground almonds (if grinding your own, do first)
¼ cup coconut flour
½ tsp. xanthan gum
8 Tbsp. unsalted butter, cut up into chunks (1 stick)
½ tsp. vanilla
Pinch of salt

Quick and easy: blend all ingredients in food processor until a ball of dough forms. Press into a 9" pie plate.

Not as quick or easy, but turns out fine: Place above ingredients into a bowl. Using a pastry cutter or fork, press ingredients into a well-blended dough. Press into a 9" pie plate.

Crumb Topping:

¼ cup ground almonds
¼ cup ground walnuts
¼ cup cold butter
1 Tbsp. honey
1 tsp. vanilla

Food processor:

If grinding whole-nuts yourself, process first. Combine above ingredients in food processor blend. Sprinkle on top of filled pie. Follow baking instructions for pie.

By Hand:

Place above ingredients into a bowl. Using a pastry cutter or fork, press ingredients into a well-blended crumbly mixture. Sprinkle on top of filled pie.
Follow baking instructions for pie.

Shopping List:

1. Almonds
2. Coconut Flour
3. Xanthan Gum
4. Unsalted Butter
5. Vanilla
6. Salt
7. Walnuts
8. Honey

Chocolate Pie Crust

2 cups ground almonds
¼ cup coconut flour
8 Tbsp. cold butter, cut up (1 stick)
2 Tbsp. cocoa powder
1 tsp. honey
½ tsp. xanthan gum
Pinch of salt

Food processor:
If grinding whole-nuts yourself, process first. Combine above ingredients in food processor until a ball of dough forms. Press into 9" pie plate. Refrigerate until ready to use or bake 10 minutes at 325° for a recipe that uses an already baked crust.

By Hand:
Place above ingredients into a bowl. Using a pastry cutter or fork, press ingredients into a well-blended dough. Press into 9" pie plate. Refrigerate until ready to use or bake 10 minutes at 325° for a recipe that uses an already baked crust.

Shopping List:

1. Almonds
2. Coconut Flour
3. Butter
4. Cocoa Powder
5. Honey
6. Xanthan Gum
7. Salt

Meringue Pie Crust

3 egg whites
¼ tsp. cream of tartar
¾ tsp. vanilla
1 Tbsp. honey
¼ tsp. xanthan gum

Place egg whites into mixing bowl. Beat on medium until starting to turn white. Add the cream of tartar, vanilla, honey, and xanthan gum. Beat on high until stiff and glossy.

<u>9" Pie Crust:</u> Pour meringue into a mound onto parchment lined cookie sheet. Using a spatula form meringue into a 9" circle with a depression in the center for the filling. Make sure the bottom is thick enough so the filling doesn't leak out when cut. Bake at 225° for 30 minutes until firm and slightly crisp. Shut off oven and leave in oven to cool slowly. Make filling while crust is baking.

<u>Mini pies:</u> Put meringue into piping bag. Pip or drop by spoonfuls onto parchment lined cookie sheet 1" in diameter circular mounds. Using a spoon scoop out a little bit to make a depression in the center of the crust for the filling. Bake at 225° for 15 minutes until firm and slightly crisp. Shut off oven and leave in oven to cool slowly. Make filling while crust is baking. Makes about 48 1" mini pies.

> <u>Tip:</u> Meringue crust pies do not store well. Plan to eat it shortly after you make it. Who doesn't want to be told to eat their dessert right now?

Shopping List:

1. Egg
2. Cream of Tartar
3. Vanilla
4. Honey
5. Xanthan Gum

Savory

Oatmeal-Garlic Cheddar Biscuits

2 cups oatmeal, ground (put oatmeal in blender to grind if not using food processor)
2 Tbsp. flax, ground
½ tsp. cream of tartar
¼ tsp. baking soda
1 Tbsp. baking powder
¼ tsp. salt
2 tsp. garlic powder

In a large bowl, add ground oatmeal, flax, cream of tartar, baking soda, baking powder, salt, and garlic powder. Combine.

½ cup shredded cheddar (a little extra to sprinkle on top too)
½ cup unsalted butter, cut into small chunks
¾ cup milk or buttermilk

Add butter. Using a pastry cutter or fork press mixture into coarse crumbs. Add milk. Stir to combine dough. Add cheese. Stir until blended. Scoop by spoonfuls onto sheet parchment lined sheet. Sprinkle with extra shredded cheddar.

Bake at 400 for 9 minutes. Makes 12 (2" biscuits)

Food Processor:
Add oatmeal to food processor. Pulse to medium consistency. Add flax, cream of tartar, baking soda, baking powder, salt, garlic powder. Pulse to mix. Add butter. Pulse to coarse crumbs. Add milk. Pulse to blend. Add cheese. Pulse until blended. Scoop by spoonfuls onto sheet parchment lined sheet. Sprinkle with extra shredded cheddar.

Bake at 400° for 9 minutes. Makes 12 (2" biscuits)

Shopping List:

1. Oatmeal
2. Flax
3. Cream of Tartar
4. Baking Soda
5. Baking Powder
6. Salt
7. Garlic Powder
8. Shredded Cheddar
9. Unsalted Butter
10. Milk or Buttermilk

Tip: To make a good buttermilk substitute add 1 Tbsp. lemon juice to ¾ cup milk. Stir. Let set for a couple of minutes before using. When I make biscuits I always use this buttermilk substitute and they are delicious!

Pizza

Crust:
10 cups shredded zucchini (frozen) (thaw and squeeze out all moisture)
dash of salt
2 eggs, beaten
1 cup mozzarella cheese (shredded)
1 cup cheddar cheese (shredded)

Mix together in large bowl. Press out thinly on greased pizza pan.

Bake at 400 for 25 minutes.

Toppings:
Pizza sauce
Veggies (onions, mushrooms, peppers, ect.)
Meat (pepperoni, sausage, bacon)
Mozzarella cheese, shredded

Spread sauce on crust. Add toppings. Cover with cheese.

Bake at 400 for 15 minutes. Makes a 16" pizza or 2 smaller pizzas.

Shopping List:
1. Shredded Zucchini
2. Salt
3. Egg
4. Mozzarella Cheese
5. Cheddar Cheese
6. Pizza Sauce
7. Veggies
8. Meat
9. Mozzarella

Garlic Parmesan Crackers

⅓ cup almond flour
⅓ cup walnut flour
⅓ cup pecan flour
¼ tsp. salt

Combine all ingredients in a bowl.

4 Tbsp. unsalted butter, melted
¼ cup cream
2 cloves minced garlic
¼ cup parmesan cheese
Garlic powder

In a small bowl, mix butter, cream, garlic, and parmesan cheese. Add flour mixture. Stir until combined. Spread on buttered sheet. Bake at 350° for 13 minutes. Sprinkle garlic powder on after baked. Cut into square after slightly cooled. Store in airtight container and refrigerate.

Shopping List:

1. Almond Flour
2. Walnut Flour
3. Pecan Flour
4. Salt
5. Unsalted Butter
6. Cream
7. Minced Garlic
8. Parmesan Cheese
9. Garlic Powder

Pancakes

3 cups oatmeal; ground
3 cups nut flour; almonds and pecans
3 Tbsp. baking powder
1 Tbsp. salt
3 Tbsp. flax seed, ground

4 cups milk
1 Tbsp. lemon juice

Add lemon juice to milk. Stir. Set aside until slightly thickened (approximately 3 minutes)

6 eggs
3/4 cup melted butter

Mix dry ingredients. Set aside. Stir soured milk into egg and butter mixture. Combine dry and wet mixtures.

1 cup whole oatmeal

Add whole oats to batter. Stir. Let set until thickened (It may take 20 minutes to thicken).

Warm griddle to 375°, do not flip until pancakes are set.

Shopping List:

1. Oatmeal
2. Almond
3. Pecan
4. Salt
5. Flax
6. Milk
7. Lemon Juice

Berry Chutney

6 cups blueberries; fresh or frozen
1 1/2 cups tart cherries; fresh or frozen
1 cup whole raspberries; fresh or frozen
1/4 cup water; approximately

Combine fruit and water in medium saucepan. Cook on high heat until the liquid begins to boil. Reduce heat to simmer. Cook until thick, stirring often to prevent scorching.

Serve hot over pancakes.

Makes approximately 4 1/2 cups

Shopping List:

1. Blueberries
2. Tart Cherries
3. Raspberries

Snacks

Plain Granola

Dry Ingredients:
2 cups sliced almonds
1 cup sunflower seeds
1 cup unsweetened coconut
1/2 cup ground flax
1/2 cup roasted & salted pistachios

In large bowl, combine above ingredients. Mix. Set aside.

Wet ingredients:
1/4 cup Earth Balance or butter, melted
1/4 cup honey
1 tsp. vanilla
1 tsp. cinnamon
Sea salt

Combine Earth Balance, honey, vanilla, and cinnamon. Pour over nut mixture. Stir until evenly coated. Spread on parchment lined sheet. Dust with sea salt. Bake at 275° for 40 minutes. Stir every 15 minutes. Allow to cool completely. Store in airtight container for up to a 1 week.

Shopping List:
1. Almonds
2. Sunflower Seeds
3. Unsweetened Coconut
4. Flax
5. Pistachios
6. Earth Balance or Butter
7. Honey
8. Vanilla
9. Cinnamon
10. Sea Salt

Chocolate Cherry Granola

Dry Ingredients:
2 cups oatmeal
1 heaping cup sliced almonds
¼ cup chopped 100% chocolate premium baking bar (4 oz.)
1 cup dried cherries (sweetened with apple juice)
½ cup ground flax

In large bowl, combine ingredients. Set aside.

Wet Ingredients:
¼ cup unsalted butter or Earth Balance, melted
¼ cup honey

Combine the butter and honey. You may need to heat slightly. Stir well.

¼ cup cocoa powder
1 tsp. vanilla
½ tsp. almond extract
Sea salt optional

Add the cocoa, vanilla, and almond extract to honey mixture. Whisk until smooth. Pour over dry ingredients. Stir until evenly coated. Spread on parchment lined sheet. Sprinkle with sea salt. Bake at 275° for 20 minutes. Allow to cool completely. Store in airtight container.

Shopping List:
1. Oatmeal
2. Almond
3. 100% Chocolate Baking Bar
4. Dried Cherries
5. Flax
6. Unsalted Butter or Earth Balance
7. Honey
8. Cocoa powder
9. Vanilla
10. Almond Extract
11. Sea Salt

Sweet and Spicy Trail Mix

1½ cups pecans (whole)
1½ cups walnuts
1 cup salted cashews
1 cup almonds
1 cup raisins
1 cup coconut

In large bowl, combine above ingredients. Set aside.

2 tsp. cumin
2 tsp. cinnamon
2 tsp. ginger
¼ tsp. cayenne Pepper

Combine spices in small bowl. Set aside.

¼ cup Earth Balance or butter
¼ cup honey
Coarse sea salt, optional

Melt butter and honey in small saucepan. Stir. Add spice mixture. Stir well. Pour over nut mixture. Stir until evenly coated. Sprinkle with coarse sea salt. Spread on parchment lined sheet. Bake at 275° for 20 minutes. Allow to cool completely. Store in airtight container.

Shopping List:

1. Pecans
2. Walnuts
3. Cashews
4. Almonds
5. Raisins
6. Coconut
7. Cumin
8. Cinnamon
9. Ginger
10. Cayenne Pepper
11. Earth Balance or Butter
12. Honey
13. Sea Salt

Cranberry Flax Granola Bars

2½ cups oatmeal
½ cups almonds, sliced
½ cups flax seed (whole)
1 cup cranberries, chopped
1 Tbsp. chia seed

Combine in large bowl. Set aside.

3 egg whites, whisked
⅓ cup honey
⅛ tsp. sea salt
½ cup butter, melted and cooled
¼ tsp. vanilla

Whisk together egg whites, honey, salt, butter, and vanilla. Pour over oatmeal mixture. Stir until combined. Spread unto parchment lined sheet. Bake at 325° for 30 min. Allow to cool slightly and then cut into bars. Store in airtight container. Refrigerate or freeze to store longer.

> **Tip:** You may need to press bars into pan to get them to act like a true granola bar.

Shopping List:

1. Oatmeal
2. Almond
3. Flax
4. Cranberries
5. Chia Seeds
6. Egg
7. Honey
8. Sea Salt
9. Butter
10. Vanilla

Chocolate Cherry Granola Breakfast Bars

2½ cups old fashion oatmeal
½ cup sliced almonds

Combine oatmeal and almonds. Pour onto parchment lined sheet. Bake at 325° for 12 minutes. Set aside.

½ cup ground flax
2 oz. 100% chocolate premium baking bar, finely chopped (½ cup)
½ cup dried cherries, chopped

In a large bowl, combine flax, cherries, and chocolate. Add cooled oatmeal mixture. Stir. Set aside.

¼ tsp. sea salt
¼ - ½ cup honey (depending on taste)
½ cup butter, melted and cooled
2 large eggs whites, lightly whisked
1 Tbsp. cocoa powder
$^1/_8$ tsp. almond extract

Combine salt, honey, butter, egg whites, cocoa, and almond extract. Pour over oatmeal-cherry mixture. Stir until combined. Spread into parchment lined sheet. Bake at 325° for 12 minutes. Allow to cool slightly and then cut into bars. Store in airtight container. Refrigerate or freeze to store longer.

> **Tip:** You may need to press bars into pan to get them to act like a true granola bar.

Shopping List:

1. Oatmeal
2. Almond
3. Flax
4. 100% Chocolate Baking Bar
5. Dried Cherries
6. Sea Salt
7. Honey
8. Butter
9. Egg
10. Cocoa Powder
11. Almond Extract

Jamie's Granola Bar

⅓ cup sliced almonds
⅓ cup pecans, chopped
⅓ cup walnuts, chopped
⅓ cup salted cashews

Place on parchment lined sheet. Bake at 325° for 6 minutes until toasted. Set aside.

½ cup coconut flakes
2 cups finely ground almond flour
pinch of sea salt
2 eggs whites, whisked
¼ tsp. vanilla
½ cup raisins, chopped

Combine vanilla and egg whites. Add coconut flakes, almond flour, salt, raisins. Mix until combined. Add nuts. Mix. Spread ¼" thick onto parchment lined sheet. Bake at 325° for 8 minutes or until firm. Do not overbake; the nuts will burn. Allow to cool and then cut into bars. Store in airtight container. Refrigerate or freeze to store longer.

>   **Tip:** You may need to press bars into pan to get them to act like a true granola bar.

Shopping List:

1. Almonds
2. Pecans
3. Walnuts
4. Cashews
5. Coconut Flakes
6. Almond Flour
7. Sea Salt
8. Egg
9. Vanilla
10. Raisins

CPSIA information can be obtained
at www.ICGtesting.com
Printed in the USA
LVHW01s0326110518
576791LV00003B/3/P